SOMERSET
The Golden Years

SOMERSET

The Golden Years

Edited by

Tom Mayberry & Hilary Binding

Somerset Books

First published in Great Britain in 2002

British Library Cataloguing-in-Publication Data
A CIP record for this title is available from the British Library

ISBN 1 86183 451 8

SOMERSET BOOKS
Official Publisher to Somerset County Council

Halsgrove House
Lower Moor Way
Tiverton, Devon EX16 6SS
Tel: 01884 243242
Fax: 01884 243325
email: sales@halsgrove.com
website: www.halsgrove.com

Printed and bound in Great Britain by Bookcraft (Bath) Ltd, Midsomer Norton

CONTENTS

Acknowledgements 6

Introduction 7

Chapter One – The Way We Were 9

Chapter Two – Land of Plenty 25

Chapter Three – Somerset and the Weather 45

Chapter Four – Enjoying Ourselves 59

Chapter Five – Getting There 75

Chapter Six – Beside the Sea 97

Chapter Seven – About Town 117

Chapter Eight – Royal Visitors 139

ACKNOWLEDGEMENTS

The great majority of the photographs contained in this book come from the extensive photographic library of the Bristol United Press. The editors are most grateful to the BUP for permission to make use of the photographs, and to Gerry Brooke for his expert guidance through the collection. For other help and information, they wish in addition to thank Steven Pugsley, Karen Binaccioni and Sharon O'Inn of Halsgrove, Ethel Carruthers, Geoff Hall, Dorothy Hardwell, Mary Hyde, Fred Johnson, Ruth Johnson and the Millennium Committee of the Norton Fitzwarren Garden Club, Christine King and Bernard Welchman.

For permission to reproduce photographs other than those from the collection of the Bristol United Press, the following are gratefully acknowledged:

Howard Drew: p. 18 (top); Elisabeth Harewood: p. 20 (top); Hulton Archive: pp. 14, 15, 16, 19, 21, 54, 60, 61, 67 (bottom), 95; M. Lockley and R.W. Pym: p. 20 (bottom); Mary Evans Picture Library: pp. 10, 13; Somerset Archive and Record Service: pp. 9, 12 (top), 17, 18 (bottom), 23, 24, 41, 59, 66, 67 (top), 75, 80 (bottom), 81, 82, 83, 129, 146 (bottom); *Somerset County Gazette*: pp. 124, 146 (top); Tom Mayberry: 12 (bottom), 58, 125.

❧ INTRODUCTION ❧

This book, published to coincide with the Queen's Golden Jubilee, provides a visual record of Somerset in the years between the end of the Second World War and the beginning of the new millennium. They were years of transformation, golden in the hopes that they inspired as the county recovered its strength in the aftermath of war, but increasingly marked by self-doubt as old patterns of living gave place to new.

Somerset emerged from the war greatly changed. Evacuees, Land Army girls and American GIs would remain vivid memories for a whole generation of Somerset people, and the scars, both human and material, inflicted by events such as the Baedeker Raids did not vanish quickly. The war had also marked the period in which Somerset farming at last emerged from a long depression. The county had responded enthusiastically to the government's wartime call to feed the nation, and by 1950 Somerset farmers were more prosperous than they had been for almost a century. In 1953, Coronation year, it seemed self-evident that agriculture was 'the most important county industry'. But already the growing numbers who worked in service industries, public administration and the tourist trade pointed to a quite different future for the county. Wassail ceremonies might continue to be held in the villages of Somerset, just as had happened in earlier times, but the forces loosening the county from its rooted, rural past were already gathering strength.

Central to the process was the rapid increase in Somerset's population. Between 1951 and 1971 the county population grew by more than 130,000 (24 per cent), and local authorities struggled to build the houses that were needed. Road traffic also grew, regularly bringing Somerset towns such as Highbridge and Taunton to a halt during the summer months. Only in 1969, when construction of the Somerset section of the M5 motorway began, was there a radical attempt to solve the problem of the motor car. But the relative calm which the M5 restored to some of the towns of Somerset was deceptive and short-lived: the county had suddenly been made more accessible than ever in its history, and was open now to social, economic and physical changes unprecedented in scale.

Of particular symbolic significance for Somerset people was the redrawing of their county boundaries following the Local Government Act of 1972. The proposals were fiercely resisted, but on 1 April 1974 the county of Somerset, more ancient as an administrative unit than England itself, was deprived of 298 square miles of its historic territory, and the unloved county of Avon began its brief existence. More than twenty years of urban growth now followed, and in Taunton alone, between 1980 and 1985, over £43m was spent on commercial development and road schemes. In the villages of Somerset, as well, change came swiftly, and the attractions of the countryside as a place to settle, not least for those in search of retirement homes, seemed irresistible. Today in West Somerset, for example, 27 per cent of the inhabitants are over sixty-five years old.

The remaking of the county in the last fifty years has not been achieved without conflict. Protection of the Levels, preservation of Exmoor, quarrying on the Mendips and disputed rights of way have been some of the many causes of great controversy. In the same years Somerset farming has declined from prosperity to deep crisis in the face of vanishing profits and, most recently, Foot and Mouth Disease. The photographs this book contains show us the many faces of Somerset during fifty transforming years, and also provide some record for the future of how the modern county was made.

Tom Mayberry
Somerset Record Office

Even the street sweeper has stopped work to ogle the new technology of television. Meadow Street, Weston-super-Mare in the 1950s.

CHAPTER ONE
~ THE WAY WE WERE ~

The years immediately before the new Queen's Coronation in 1953 marked the period in which the foundations of modern Somerset were laid. Attlee's Government, elected in the Labour landslide of 1945, introduced a series of far-reaching reforms, including the Agriculture Act of 1947 and the creation of the National Health Service in the following year. Time-honoured customs, such as wassailing the apple trees and egg shackling on Shrove Tuesday, were still faithfully observed. But the future, for the moment, seemed more attractive than the past. Workers from the Van Heusen factory in Taunton saw a vision of that future when they visited the Festival of Britain in 1951. And two years later the Coronation itself, watched by millions on newly-acquired television sets, was a symbol of hope after the dark years of war.

A Christmas gathering in a Cheddar pub during the 1940s.

Villagers gather in a Carhampton orchard during the 1940s for the wassail ceremony. By tradition the ceremony took place on Old Christmas Eve (5 January) or Old Twelfth Night (17 January) in expectation of plenty during the coming year. Toast for the robins was placed in the branches of the oldest apple tree, cider was poured around it roots, shotguns were fired to frighten away evil spirits, and the wassail song was sung.

Holidays at home! The Bandstand in the Jubilee Gardens at Minehead in 1946. A concert party performs to a thin crowd.

A ballet performance at Grove Park, Weston-super-Mare, during August 1945. All free, including the deck-chairs.

Taunton, once a bastion of Conservatism, was claimed by Labour in the landslide of 1945. The seat was won by Victor Collins, seen here second from right at the County Hotel in Taunton in 1948. With him are *(left to right)* Jack Humphrey, County Organiser of the National Union of Agricultural Workers, Earl Waldegrave, the Rt Hon. Tom Williams, Minister of Agriculture and Fisheries, and Jo Gilling, County Chairman of the Somerset NFU.

Mary Street, Taunton, before it was widened to create an inner bypass, around 1955.

Egg shackling at Stoke St Gregory in about 1950. On Shrove Tuesday eggs were brought to school by the children, inscribed with their names. The eggs were gently shaken in a sieve until only one remained unbroken.

Wild Exmoor ponies from Somerset and Devon are rounded up at Bampton for auction, 10 November 1945.

Patients crowd the waiting room of the village surgery at Williton, 1948, the year in which the National Health Service came into existence. This remarkable photograph, and the one which follows, were the work of the émigré photographer Erich Auerbach.

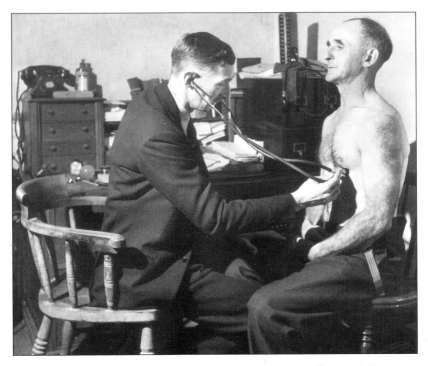

A doctor listens to his patient's heart in the surgery at Williton, 1948.

Children at Lovington School say their prayers, watched by their teacher Miss Walrond, 15 July 1948.

The gathering in of the harvest, above the church at Norton Fitzwarren in 1949. (This is now the Hill Fort picnic area.)

Winston Churchill at the Empire Hall, Taunton, 8 February 1950. Taunton had been won by the Labour Party in the landslide election of 1945, and Churchill was in Taunton to rally support for the Conservative candidate, Henry Hopkinson. At the election held two weeks later Hopkinson duly took the seat.

Members of the Stoke St Mary Women's Institute gather in the village hall to celebrate their 21st anniversary, 1953.

Workers from the Van Heusen shirt factory in Taunton arrive at Paddington Station, London, on their way to the Festival of Britain, 2 June 1951.

The Mayor of Yeovil meets the parents of childen born on Coronation Day, 2 June 1953.

Villagers at Buckland St Mary gather in the school for the Coronation dinner, June 1953.

Two elderly residents of Hinton St George pause in the village street to discuss the Coronation, 3 June 1953. This photograph first appeared in *Picture Post*.

Residents of Axbridge celebrate the Coronation in the town square, 2 June 1953.

SUNDAY, MAY 31st.

A UNITED SERVICE ON THE CRICKET FIELD

(by kind permission of W. Palmer, Esq.)

Conducted by the Rector : REV. W. E. MORGAN, at 3 p.m.

(If wet, the Service will be held in the Parish Church)

During the Service, the children of the Parish will be presented with a *Coronation Souvenir Bible*, by W. C. PARKHOUSE, Esq., Chairman of the Parish Council.

MONDAY, JUNE 1st.

A SHORT INFORMAL SERVICE OF VIGIL
BEFORE THE CORONATION, at 9.0 p.m.

in the Parish Church, in response to the Queen's wish that we all pray for her.

TUESDAY, JUNE 2nd.

SPORTS FOR THE CHILDREN
In the War Memorial Playing Field.

JUNIORS at 4 p.m.   SENIORS at 5 p.m.

CORONATION TEA FOR THE CHILDREN
At the County Primary School.

SENIORS at 4 p.m.   JUNIORS at 5 p.m.

ADULT SPORTS
at 6 p.m.   GOOD PRIZES.

Programme for Coronation celebrations at West Huntspill, 1953. On Coronation Day, 2 June, everyone gathered in the Balliol Hall to watch the day's events on television.

The Market House, Taunton, decorated for the Queen's Coronation, June 1953. Some of the same decorations were used when the Queen visited the town for her Golden Jubilee in May 2002.

Hammet Street, Taunton, decorated for the Coronation.

CHAPTER TWO
❧ LAND OF PLENTY ❧

Despite the crisis which overtook Somerset agriculture in the late 1990s, and from which it has not yet emerged, farming was largely prosperous during the second half of the twentieth century. The farming slump which many had feared after the Second World War did not occur, and the mechanisation made necessary by wartime demands continued rapidly when peace returned. The most representative photograph included here shows a combine harvester on a farm near Yeovil. Several photographs look back to a time that was gone even when they were taken – a time of plough teams and Fordson tractors, stooks of wheat and straw for thatching. Others relate to once prevalent activities, such as cider and cheese making, which are now the specialist preserve of the few.

A team of horses at work on Mrs D.E.B. Crumpler's farm, East Coker, in about 1950.

Stoney Street, Luccombe, as it appeared in the 1940s, recreated for television in the 1980s.

Harvesting wheat at Seavington St Michael, August 1976. The straw is destined for thatching, and for that reason the crop is stooked and lifted by tractor and trailer.

Harvesting in the traditional way at Ashe Farm, Thornfalcon, during the 1970s. The farmer, David Small (second left), supplied the straw for thatching.

Brian Johnson from Pymore, near Bridport, on his 1942 Fordson tractor keeps an eye on his line during the Ploughing Match at Chiselborough, September 1985.

Ian Grant from Wrantage, near Taunton, with his father's winning entry in the vintage tractor class at the Chiselborough Ploughing Match, September 1985.

Combining oats at Newton Farm, near Yeovil, August 1978.

Experienced onlookers consider the finer points at Tor Fair, Glastonbury, September 1976. The auctioneer is Mr Digby of Wells.

Priddy Fair, 1996.

Judging time in the Suffolk sheep classes at Dunster Show, August 1995.

Mr Harry Cook of Staplegrove Mills, Taunton, wins the supreme championship at Taunton Fatstock Show, December 1983, with Prince Charming, a fourteen-month-old Angus–cross steer. With him is the Mayor of Taunton Deane, Councillor Lewis Lane.

Pauline Carnell from Mark, a member of Wedmore Young Farmers' Club, with a Limousin-cross, winner of four classes at Highbridge Fatstock Show, December 1990.

Henry Tinney's Charolais–cross Friesian calf was the last animal to be sold before Glastonbury Market closed for the final time in March 1989. Mr Tinney, of Cradlebridge, Glastonbury, had long family connections with Glastonbury Market. His grandfather, George, bought the first cow and calf sold at the market when it moved to its purpose–built site in 1908.

The Mayor of Taunton Deane, Councillor Ernest Warren, sells the first steer at the reopened Tuesday Fatstock Market in Taunton, April 1981. The market had been closed during the previous year through lack of support.

The banner of the former National Union of Agricultural Workers in Somerset was carried through the streets of Glastonbury in October 1984 before being laid up in the Somerset Rural Life Museum. The procession was led by Mr Jack Humphrey *(standing on cart, right)*, who raised £100 in 1949 to buy the silk banner. Mr Humphrey appears over thirty years earlier in the top photograph on p.12. Also pictured is Mr Percy Dando, chairman of the county branch in 1949.

Members of Mendip Young Farmers' Club at their last annual rally before being merged with other sections in the new Fosse branch, May 1995. Pictured are the group from Farrington Gurney.

Warnings of Foot and Mouth disease at a farm near Yeovil, March 1981.

Strawberry picking in the Mendips, June 1968.

Loading the Strawberry Special at Draycott Station, June 1964. The fruit was sent to wholesalers across the country.

Charles Clive-Ponsonby-Fane, with helpers, harvesting the grape crop from his one-acre vineyard at Brympton D'Evercy, Yeovil, November 1977.

Harry Ware and Robert Routley making cider at the Cottage Inn, Fiddington in about 1950.

The Press Room 'Gang', Taunton Cider Company, Norton Fitzwarren, 1958.

Apple Day celebrations, October 1999.

The first pint of Butcombe Brewery's new 'Wilmot's Premium Ale' was pulled at the Bell Inn, Hillgrove Street, Bristol, by Gavin Whitmee, grandson of the head brewer, John Wilmot, after whom the beer was named, June 1996. The brewery, near Blagdon, began production in 1978.

Cheese judges Roy Hawker and Jimmy Wilson with committee member Stan Reeves *(left)* at Frome Cheese Show, September 1996.

Fears of pollution at Blagdon Lake in March 1996 brought inspectors to the scene. The lake had been stocked with 10,000 fish for the launch of the new season but many had been found dead.

CHAPTER THREE
SOMERSET AND THE WEATHER

T he weather has always been a preoccupation for Somerset people, and extremes of weather have regularly marked the fifty years since the Queen came to the throne. In August 1952, the worst flash floods Britain has ever experienced swept through the villages of Exmoor, taking the lives of 35 people at Lynmouth, and in July 1968 floods caused widespread damage. Violent storms have often struck the Somerset coast, and winter floodwaters are a frequent sight on the Somerset Levels. Only snowdrifts are now less familiar than they were to earlier generations, but winter gales blow stronger, or so it seems, and on 25 January 1990 they caused devastation throughout the West Country.

A storm on the sea front at Weston-super-Mare, January 1962.

March 1980. Giant waves crash over the sea wall at Minehead as gale-force winds combine with the second highest tide of the winter. Cottages in Quay Street were flooded and damaged.

Work in progress on the new sea wall at Brean, June 1983. A similar wall was built at Burnham.

Work in progress to restore the harbour wall at Watchet, April 1981.

Fireman on Clevedon sea front in February 1990 begin to clear railings brought down by high winds.

Friends and workmen rescue furnishings from the Golden Guernsey Milk Bar near the bridge at Dulverton, devastated in the same floods that caused the disaster at Lynmouth in August 1952.

Wading through the floods at Taunton, October 1960.

Following flooding at Taunton in October 1960, many Taunton sweetshops threw away condemned stocks. Local youngsters were not deterred and began an unofficial salvage operation.

Freak floods in Cheddar Gorge, July 1968. The whole county was severely affected by flooding.

The aftermath of the floods in Cheddar Gorge, July 1968. The force of the water brought down tons of debris and caused much damage.

Flooding at Southlake Moor, February 1980.

Floods at Curload, Stoke St Gregory, 1993.

Burrow Mump rises above the floods in February 1995. The A361 just remains passable, but most minor roads in the area are under water.

In the winter of 1962–63 some sheep on Exmoor were saved from starvation by the work of the RAF air-rescue in delivering bales of hay to where they are situated on the moors. Villagers seen here have helped load the hay into the aircraft.

A snowplough at work on the Mendips, December 1964.

Skiing to work through the snow-covered streets of Taunton, February 1978.

Sudden snowstorms swept the West Country on 22 November 1993, leaving many minor roads and some major ones impassable until the snowploughs arrived.

Councillor Derrick Lovering negotiates a pool of mud on a footpath near the Triangle at Clevedon, April 1987.

The road outside St Thomas's Church, Thurlbear, following the great storm of 25 January 1990.

The Tithe Barn at Thurlbear after being struck by a tree during the great gale of 25 January 1990.

CHAPTER FOUR
~ ENJOYING OURSELVES ~

Whether re-enacting a Viking raid, watching Somerset at the County Ground or playing on a swing hanging from a Mendip signpost, Somerset people have never lacked resourcefulness in finding ways to enjoy themselves. Events such as Somerset's many carnivals have deep roots in local communities, and the most famous of them, at Bridgwater, traces its origins to the 1850s. The Glastonbury Pop Festival is a more recent creation and has quickly become a world-famous annual attraction. It was founded by Michael and Jean Eavis at Worthy Farm, Pilton, in 1970, when 1500 people were present. By 1998 the attendance had reached 100,000.

The ladies' skittle team, Norton Fitzwarren, in fancy dress, January 1951.

Robert Parry, aged twelve, pushes Andrew Johns on a home-made swing hanging from a road sign in Chewton Mendip, 2 May 1952.

Children wearing shoes made by Clark's of Street, July 1955. The firm were testing the durability of children's footwear and gave a pair of shoes to every child in the town, with instructions to treat the shoes exactly as they pleased.

A fun run sets off from Ashton Court, Long Ashton, in April 1991.

Some of the 1600 Somerset schoolchildren who took part in the annual folk dancing event at Wells, June 1980.

The Rt Revd Jim Thompson, Bishop of Bath and Wells, signals the start of the annual raft race in the moat of the Bishop's Palace, Wells, July 1993. Under the rules, every team in the race must contain a member of the clergy. The winners were St Andrew's Church, Congresbury. The raft belonging to the Wells Ladies' Circle sank.

A re-enactment in July 1988 of a Viking raid on Watchet one thousand years earlier.

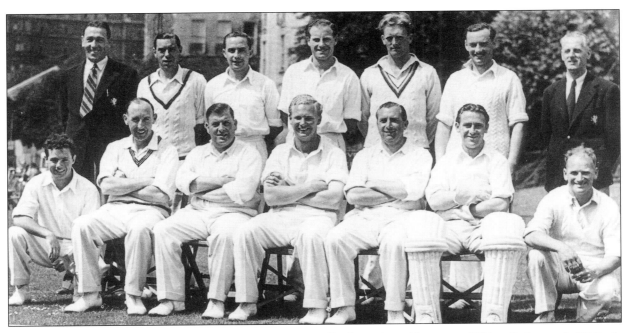

The Somerset Cricket Team photographed for Arthur Wellard's testimonial season, 1951. *Back row*: A. Wellard, E. Robinson, L. Angell, J. Redman, M. Tremlett, F. Irish and R. Trump (scorer). *Front Row*: R. Smith, H. Buse, H. Hazell, S. Rogers (captain), H. Gimblett, H. Stephenson and J. Lawrence.

The Somerset Team in 1978, the year before they won the Gillette Cup. *Back Row*: Keith Jennings, Hallam Moseley, Peter Roebuck, Joel Garner, Colin Dredge, Ian Botham, Vic Marks and Phil Slocombe. *Front Row*: Neil Russom, Graham Burgess, Peter Denning, Brian Rose (captain), Derek Taylor, Viv Richards and Dennis Breakwell.

Viv Richards and Ian Botham.

Bath Rugby Club (in white) takes on Bridgwater Rugby Club, 7 December 1946.

WORTHY FARM
TWINNED WITH
SCORAIG

SALE & DISPLAY OF
DRUGS FORBIDDEN

TICKET
CHECKPOINT

← PARKING ONLY
TRADERS →
↓ CAMPING

At the entrance to the Glastonbury Pop Festival, Pilton, June 1984.

Crowds at the Glastonbury Pop Festival in the early 1970s.

A dancer at the Glastonbury Pop Festival, 1971, the festival's second year.

Life inside a polythene tepee at the Glastonbury Pop Festival, June 1971.

Traffic at the site of the Glastonbury Pop Festival, June 1984.

Michael Eavis, who in 1970 founded the Glastonbury Pop Festival at Worthy Farm, Pilton, helps to clear up.

The main stage at the Glastonbury Pop Festival, June 1990.

The Tower of London and Yeomen of the Guard depicted in a float for Bridgwater Carnival, 1959.

Flower Power inspires an entry, called 'the Loco Ono Band', at Chard Carnival, 1969.

A float called 'Currency Capers' at Chard Carnival, 1970, commemorates the last days of pounds, shillings and pence.

The Chard Reservoir Monster makes an appearance at Chard Carnival, 1971.

The days of empire are remembered in a float at Ilminster Carnival, 1977.

Tor Fair lights up the night sky at Glastonbury in about 1980.

CHAPTER FIVE
❧ GETTING THERE ❧

The new Elizabethan Age has been dominated not least by the motor car. It has clogged the centres of Somerset towns, forced the adoption of controversial road schemes, and, of course, provided the inhabitants of a very rural county with a degree of mobility unknown to earlier generations. The building of the M5 motorway, completed to Exeter in 1977, was a watershed in Somerset history and opened the county to the greater world as never before. By the time it was finished, steam trains were little more than a memory, and the routes targeted by Dr Beeching had already vanished from the timetables.

Len Webber delivering bread at Norton Fitzwarren in about 1960.

Police Sergeant Rod Price with his bicycle in Axbridge Town Square, November 1978.

Holiday traffic pours through Taunton at the start of the summer holidays, July 1953.

Traffic chaos in the centre of Wells, April 1992.

Only one passenger turned up when a special bus service was launched on Exmoor in May 1976. The Land Rover, driven by Mrs May Collins, a farmer's wife, was intended to replace the buses once linking remote rural settlements with Minehead.

Minibuses had replaced the Bristol Omnibus Company's double-deckers in the Weston-super-Mare area by April 1988. Plans were also in hand to introduce minibuses on some Bristol routes.

A timber lorry comes to grief below the first bend of Porlock Hill in September 1978.

Open countryside near Clevedon before work began on the M5 motorway in 1971. The scene shows Crook Peak and the Webbington Hotel.

Starting work on the Clevedon Hills section of the M5 motorway, 1970.

The Clevedon Hills section of the M5 motorway following completion, 1973.

Construction of the Wynhol Viaduct on the M5 motorway near Clevedon, about 1972.

Building the Chelston junction of the M5 motorway near Wellington, 1973.

W.T.F. Austin, the Project Manager, shakes hands with the Prime Minister, the Rt Hon. James Callaghan, at the Exeter opening of the M5 motorway, 27 May 1977.

Steam on the Cheddar Valley Line near Axbridge, April 1962.

The Cheddar Valley Line, 1960.

The platform at Draycott Station, April 1961.

Clifford Miller waves off the last train on the Taunton to Yeovil line, June 1964.

The last train on the Taunton to Yeovil line makes its way across country, June 1964.

Crowds gather for a last train excursion on the Taunton to Barnstaple line before it was closed at the beginning of October 1966.

A driver's-eye view of the Taunton to Barnstaple line taken a few days before its closure, October 1966.

One house had a lucky escape when part of the railway viaduct at Waterloo Road, Shepton Mallet, collapsed in February 1946.

The line between Chard and Taunton was dismantled in 1965.

The station at Weston-super-Mare in March 1984. The days of steam are long gone.

Ships on the River Parrett at Bridgwater, January 1969.

Two 30-ton sections of Bridgwater's 140-year-old bascule bridge, restored at a cost of £180,000, are put back in place by a giant crane, 1983: a major step in restoring Bridgwater Docks, last used for shipping in the 1960s, and closed in 1971.

Richard Hyde, Commodore of the Conservators of the River Tone, presides at the reopening of the Bridgwater and Taunton Canal, June 1994. A major restoration of the canal had just been completed.

Britain's most advanced and biggest hovercraft, the Westland SRN 2, ready to leave its hangar for initial engine trials in the Solent, June 1963.

Two Westland 'Puma' helicopters in army camouflage flying over Yeovil in about 1970.

Crowds at the Balloon Fiesta watch Concorde make a low-level pass over Ashton Court, Long Ashton, August 1986.

CHAPTER SIX
〜 BESIDE THE SEA 〜

Ever since Minehead in the 1790s was advertised as a tourist resort, and Samuel Taylor Coleridge went swimming in the sea at Clevedon, Somerset has prized its sea coast as a place of recreation. Weston-super-Mare, which acquired its first hotel as early as 1808, was dominated by the tourist trade before the end of the nineteenth century, and in the 1980s was welcoming 350,000 holiday-makers a year. It was at Brean, a short distance down the coast, that Fred Pontin invented the holiday camp in 1946, and at Minehead that Billy Butlin created the camp now called Somerwest World in 1962. Not all Somerset's seaside visitors have necessarily been welcome: Weston in the 1970s was a regular Bank Holiday destination for Bristol skinheads.

The Punch and Judy man entertains the children at Weston-super-Mare on August Bank Holiday, 1960.

Aerial view of the crowds at Weston–super–Mare on Whit Monday, 1959.

Holiday–makers at Anchor Head, Weston–super–Mare, August 1959.

Visitors crowd the beach at Weston-super-Mare in about 1975.

The pool at Weston-super-Mare in the late-1970s. It was demolished in 1981.

The Yacht Club Regatta in Weston-super-Mare Bay, May 1964.

Jean Murphy (centre), Dolores Powell (right) and Joy Gill (left), finalists in the Modern
Venus competition, Weston-super-Mare, 1952. With them is the music hall performer
Old Mother Riley (Arthur Lucan).

John Cleese with Deidre Greenland, winner of the second round of the Modern Venus competition, Weston-super-Mare, July 1972.

Children visiting Weston–super–Mare's model village, 1962.

The Weston-super-Mare pop group The Iveys after a five-week tour in Sweden, September 1965.

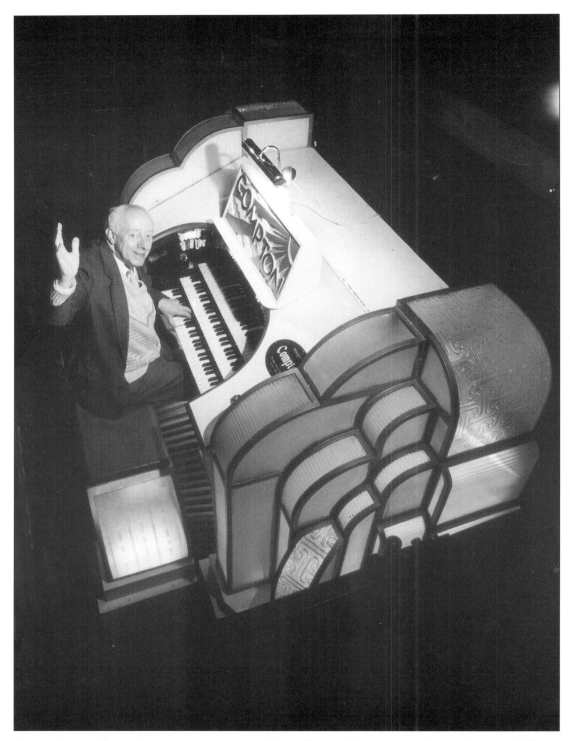

Trevor Dean with the Compton organ in the Odeon Cinema, Weston-super-Mare, October 1995.

The amusement arcade on Weston-super-super-Mare's Grand Pier, August 1988. Children who were asked their opinion of the pier and the arcade said they liked the adventure playground, but thought the Crazy House was 'totally naff'.

Weston–super–Mare was for several years a regular destination for Bristol skinheads. Here a policeman conducts a search at the town's station, 1971.

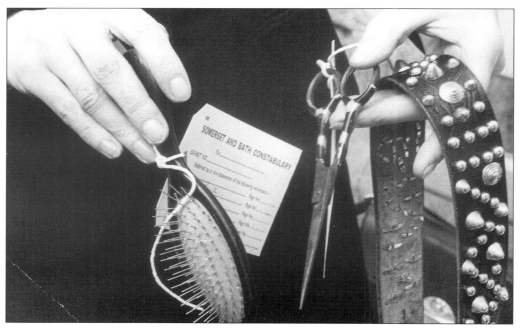

Some of the potential weapons confiscated from skinheads arriving at Weston–super–Mare, 1971.

Trouble breaks out at Weston–super–Mare on Easter Monday, 1970.

Arrests are made at Weston–super–Mare, August 1970.

An early photograph of the holiday centre at Brean created by Fred Pontin in 1946.

Sir Fred Pontin, aged eighty-nine, returns to the holiday camp at Brean from which his empire grew, May 1996. In 1946 Sir Fred borrowed £23,000 to buy a former army barracks at Brean and to convert it into a holiday centre.

Work begins on dismantling the pierhead of Clevedon Pier a decade after the Victorian structure partially collapsed in 1970.

Crowds gather for the reopening of Clevedon Pier following its restoration, 1991.

The sea front at Burnham-on-Sea, May 1973.

Visitors walk along the new sea defences at Burnham-on-Sea, September 1985.

The Weston-super-Mare lifeboat *Fifi and Charles* rescues sea cadets off Clevedon, August 1957.

The crew of Minehead motor lifeboat, May 1973.

A view of Watchet Harbour, September 1980.

The harbour at Porlock Weir, September 1971.

The monorail at the Butlin's holiday camp, Minehead, during the 1980s.

Rod Hull and Emu at the opening of a new swimming pool at Butlin's, Minehead, 1984.

Lifeguards test the new water slides at Somerwest World (formerly Butlin's), Minehead, April 1986. The holiday camp had just been given a £10m upgrading and a new name.

CHAPTER SEVEN
~ ABOUT TOWN ~

The towns of Somerset, and the city of Wells, have been essential economic and social components in the life of the county since the Middle Ages. Scattered from Frome to Dulverton, and from Minehead to Crewkerne, most have retained their essential character as small market centres, providing a focus for the immediate territory in which they stand. But others have outgrown their origins during the last fifty years, and Taunton especially is rapidly acquiring a regional significance. The photographs included here show a few of the scenes, occupations, personalities and events that went to the making of Somerset towns in the late-twentieth century.

View of Fore Street, Dulverton, looking towards All Saints' Church, September 1977.

The bridge over the River Barle at Dulverton, 1961. Contrast this with the aftermath of the 1952 flood (p.48) when the Milk Bar that adjoined the row of houses on the left of this picture was so badly damaged it had to be demolished.

The Dulverton Friendly Society, gathered outside the Market House, meet for the last time, September 1968.

A torchlight procession at Chard in January 1985 to mark the 750th anniversary of the creation of the Borough of Chard.

A view along Market Street, Crewkerne, in May 1974.

The bronze statue of Admiral Robert Blake, Bridgwater's most famous son, is hoisted from its site outside the Market House before being fixed on a new plinth 25 yards away, March 1986. A crowd of nearly 500 watched the controversial operation.

Demolition work in February 1984 led to the discovery of foundations belonging to Bridgwater's long-vanished castle. The picture shows Peter Ellis of the Western Archaeological Trust, and Mike Blake of the demolition contractors, at the north wall of the castle.

A busy day in East Street, Taunton, in about 1985.

North Street, Taunton, looking towards the Market House during the 1960s.

The west wall of Taunton's fifteenth-century Guildhall was revealed in February 1996 as a result of work relating to the Town Centre Enhancement Scheme.

The Market House and the Burma War Memorial, Taunton, following the reorganisation of the town centre, 1996.

St Margaret's Hospital, Taunton, becomes the victim of an arson attack in September 1992. Restoration of the building was only finally completed in 2002.

The Odeon Cinema, Taunton, in its heyday, September 1955. The building was demolished and the site redeveloped in 1999.

The skeleton of Taunton's new five-screen cinema rises at Hankridge Farm in February 1994.

Temples old and new: the tower of St Mary's Church, Taunton, the grandest and greatest of Somerset church towers, and the Safeway supermarket in 1998.

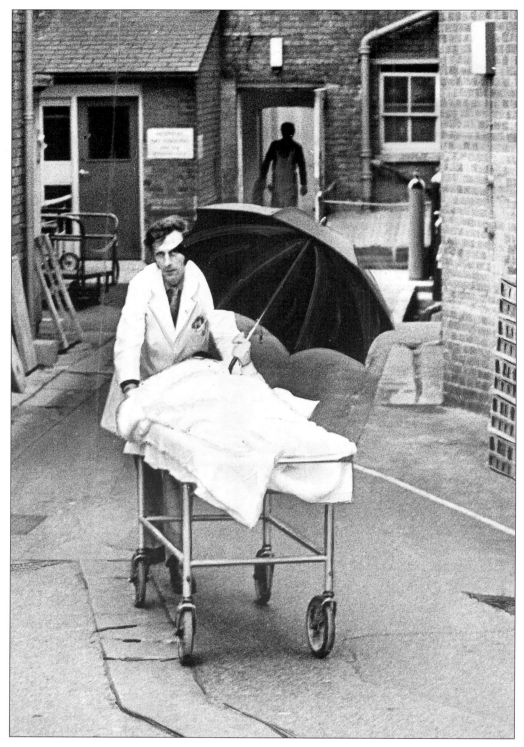

A patient being taken to the X-ray department at East Reach Hospital, Taunton, uses an umbrella to shield herself from the rain, 1975.

Activity time in the lounge at Trinity Hospital, Taunton, during the 1980s. Many of the elderly patients never forgot that the hospital occupied the premises of Taunton's former workhouse.

Workers at the Unicorn Shirt Co-operative in Taunton celebrate the firm's first birthday, October 1982. Redundant shirt workers were given rent-free use of the factory for a year by their former employer, the Luvisca Shirt Company.

The Bishop of Clifton leads the Stations of the Cross at Glastonbury in the presence of Cardinal Basil Hume and other clergy, June 1979.

A cutting taken from the Holy Thorn is received by the Mayor of Glastonbury, December 1987.

In January 1992 fire destroyed part of the abandoned Moorland's factory complex on the outskirts of Glastonbury. The site remains derelict ten years later.

The Rt Revd Edward Henderson, Bishop of Bath and Wells, in the Market Place at Wells, June 1975.

The Chairman of Somerset County Council, Councillor Bill Meadows, unveils a Civic Trust award plaque commemorating the restoration of the medieval Vicars' Close, Wells, April 1985. The restoration lasted a decade and cost more than £300,000.

Les Tracey outside the Regal Cinema in Wells. After his plans to turn the cinema into a nightclub were rejected he put the building up for sale.

Ron Wilkey prepares lengths of horsehair for weaving at John Boyd Textiles, Castle Cary, about 1980. Boyd's has remained the only manufacturer of horsehair fabrics in Britain.

Francis Showering opens the new Shepton Mallet Centre (now the Amulet) in the Market Place, Shepton Mallet, December 1975. The new building contained a theatre and other facilities. In 1953 Francis Showering began distribution of his new invention, Babycham, from his factory in Shepton Mallet.

A view of the Market Place at Frome in February 1976.

A march through the centre of Weston–super–Mare protesting against the threatened closure of the Westland's helicopter factory in the town, April 1987.

The remains of a giant chimney at Portishead Power Station are brought down in June 1982, nine months after the major part of the 350ft-high stack was blown up.

CHAPTER EIGHT
~ ROYAL VISITORS ~

Though Somerset was not always the most loyal of counties, royal visitors have been frequent during the last fifty years. The Queen Mother, who, with the King, visited Bath soon after the Baedeker Raids in 1942, returned many times. So too did the Princess of Wales. Prince Charles, whose Duchy of Cornwall estates include much land in Somerset, has visited often and has expressed a 'very special personal affection' for the cathedral at Wells. A visit by the Queen to rebellious Taunton in 1987 dispelled the long-held belief that no reigning monarch would ever set foot in a town that had proclaimed the Duke of Monmouth king. For good measure, she visited Taunton again in May 2002 at the beginning of her Golden Jubilee tour.

In March 1960 the Queen Mother visited Bath. Here she is seen being driven along the Royal Crescent, cheered by crowds of Bath schoolchildren, on her way to the Domestic Science College.

A visit to Bath in March 1963 included a stop at the Assembly Rooms.

The Royal Bath and West Show, June 1976. The Queen Mother presents an award to Marion Mould.

The Queen Mother presents Colours at Bath in October 1979.

The Queen Mother arrives in Wells, July 1979. She is accompanied by Lt Col. Walter Luttrell.

The Queen Mother plants a tree to mark her visit to Wells Cathedral School, July 1979.

Happy faces show how much pleasure the Queen Mother's visit to Wells gave to young and old.

Weston–super–Mare decorated with bunting and banners to mark the Queen Mother's eightieth birthday on 4 August 1980.

On her visit to Wells in July 1985 the Queen Mother had a congratulatory word for Arthur Culliford, aged 103.

During a royal visit to Weston-super-Mare in December 1986 the Queen was welcomed by Cub Scouts during a walkabout.

In May 1987 the Queen came to Somerset. In Taunton (*top*) she became the first reigning monarch to visit the town since 1497. In Norton Fitzwarren (*bottom*) she was greeted by local children.

On the same day she also visited Bridgwater and was welcomed by large crowds.

In April 1993 the traditional Maundy service was held at Wells Cathedral. The Queen presented Maundy money to 41 elderly people, the number equivalent to the years of her reign.

After the Maundy ceremony at Wells in 1993 Prince Philip lifts a small child over the heads of the crowd so that she can present a posy of flowers to the Queen.

Prince Charles at the Royal Naval base at Yeovilton in November 1974. On the left, Vice Admiral Peter Austin, Flag Officer Naval Air Command, explains a point while Captain James Phillips, Commanding Officer, looks on.

Prince Charles at the controls of a Royal Navy helicopter at Yeovil during his three months' training in the autumn of 1974.

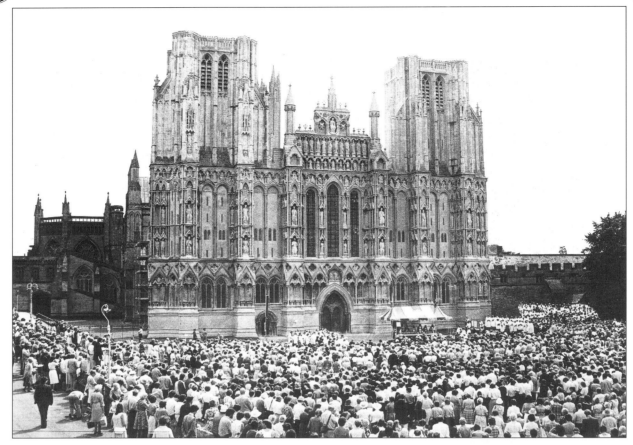

In June 1986 Prince Charles joined more that 4000 worshippers at a communion service at Wells Cathedral to give thanks for the completion of the restoration of the West Front.

Prince Charles visits Westland's, Yeovil, in 1989 and congratulates them on their outstanding achievements.

Prince Charles tries out a chair at the opening of workshops in North Street, Stoke sub Hamdon, converted from farm buildings, October 1985.

Princess Diana talks to children during her visit to Midsomer Norton in November 1982. She and Prince Charles were hosts to 140 tenants and staff of the Duchy of Cornwall at the Fosseway Country Club.

Princess Diana visits Glastonbury, April 1984.

Princess Diana greets children in the crowd at Glastonbury, oblivious that the barriers may be giving way. The police are more concerned.

Princess Diana, the People's Princess. Taunton, June 1993.

Princess Anne meets a group of majorettes in Shepton Mallet, April 1987. She was the town's first royal visitor for forty years and was there to open the new headquarters of Mendip District Council.

Princess Anne visiting Whatley Quarry, October 1987.

On a visit to Yeovil and Ilchester in July 1988 Princess Anne accepts a bunch of flowers from a young admirer.

Two days later she enjoyed all the fun of the fair at Burnham-on-Sea.

The Vice Lieutenant of Somerset, Lt Col. Walter Luttrell, accompanies the Duchess of Kent from a service in Wells Cathedral, in September 1970.

Princess Alexandra opening the Phoenix Mill of the Wansborough Paper Company, Watchet, November 1977.

In September 1986 Prince Andrew began an eighteen-week residential helicopter warfare instructor's course at the Royal Naval Air Station at Yeovilton. He is seen arriving on his first day.